JAMAICA BAY    PHYSICAL MODELS

JAMAICA BAY PAMPHLET LIBRARY 16

# JAMAICA BAY PHYSICAL MODELS

## STRUCTURES OF COASTAL RESILIENCE

Jamaica Bay Team
Spitzer School of Architecture
The City College of New York

Catherine Seavitt Nordenson, editor
Associate Professor of Landscape Architecture

Kjirsten Alexander
Research Associate

Danae Alessi
Research Associate

Eli Sands
Research Assistant

JAMAICA BAY PAMPHLET LIBRARY
16 Jamaica Bay Physical Models

ISBN 978-1-942900-16-0

COPYRIGHT

CONTACT
Catherine Seavitt Nordenson
cseavittnordenson@ccny.cuny.edu
www.structuresofcoastalresilience.org

SCR Jamaica Bay Team
The City College of New York
Spitzer School of Architecture
Program in Landscape Architecture, Room 2M24A
141 Convent Avenue New York, New York 10031

COVER
Continuous surface CNC milled model of Jamaica Bay

supported by

THE ROCKEFELLER FOUNDATION

SCR
Structures of Coastal Resilience

CUNY
The City University of New York

The City College of New York

## HYDRAULIC MODELS AND THE WATER TANK

Scale models of watersheds, river basins, and bays, deployed performatively in water tanks for empirical hydrodynamic analyses, have been used for decades. Hydraulic physical models were developed most notably by the Waterways Experiment Station (WES) of the United States Army Corps of Engineers. The scalar Mississippi River Basin Model, whose construction began in 1943, covered more than 800 acres of land; its surface was literally flooded with water to simulate conditions of the 1953 and 1973 floods. It was also used to predict flooding and to test flood control barriers. Other WES hydraulic models, such as the New York Harbor Model, the San Francisco Bay Model, and the Chesapeake Bay Model, studied sedimentation and salt water intrusion.

Since the 1960s, many of the hydraulic models and water tanks have been abandoned by fluid dynamicists and civil engineers in favor of computational fluid dynamics modelling programs such as Advanced Circulation (ADCIRC) and other finite-element method digital simulations. This trend toward digital modelling follows a similar philosophical shift that understands the

New York Harbor Model
source: US Army Corps of Engineers, Waterways Experiment Station

physical containment of water flow—the riverbed or estuarine bathymetry—as an unchanging, unmoving, clearly delineated vessel; that is, a channel. This non-complex trough, in which no sedimentation or meander is presumed, readily adapts itself to the two-dimensional digital model.

However, there is renewed interest, particularly from designers, in the use of the simple hydraulic water tank as a testing instrument and research tool, as it captures a more complex and dynamic set of variables than the concrete design heights and widths of this two-dimensional channel philosophy. The USACE paradigm shift in coastal resiliency is the increased interest in natural and nature-based features such as constructed reefs, wetlands, and barrier islands. These "soft infrastructures" have the potential to transform the water's velocity, reduce fetch, capture and retain floodwaters, and collect or redirect sediment. As these natural systems are enhanced as part of a coastal storm risk management strategy, the potential of the water tank as an experimental design tool is extremely rich.

Mississippi River Basin Model
source: US Army Corps of Engineers, Waterways Experiment Station

Jamaica Bay Topobathy Model, detail of Breezy Point and Rockaway Inlet, looking north-east

## PHYSICAL MODELING AT JAMAICA BAY

The SCR Jamaica Bay team has developed a detailed
morphology of Jamaica Bay, from the regional scale of the
watershed to local features within the embayment, through the
use of physical models. Model construction methods include
topographic contour models, glycerine soap casts of inverse
contour models, and continuous-surface topobathy Computer
Numerical Control (CNC) milled models. These physical models
are deployed in water tanks with injected dye to test the dynamic
conditions of water flow, residence time, overwash, sediment
transfer, and surge. The water tank studies have provided
integral feedback to the design process at the full scale of the
embayment as well as at detailed areas of interest.

The use of the water tank as an experimental design tool allows
visualization of the patterns of current and sediment flow, as
well as a performative assessment of form-making. We seek
to understand sediment—both its flow and capture—under the
influence of tidal movement and wave velocity, and to study how
the strategic enhancement of natural processes might produce a
more resilient coastline. The hydraulic water tank models vividly
illustrate sediment transport and the forces of trailing eddies,
wakes, and vortices.

Jamaica Bay model construction

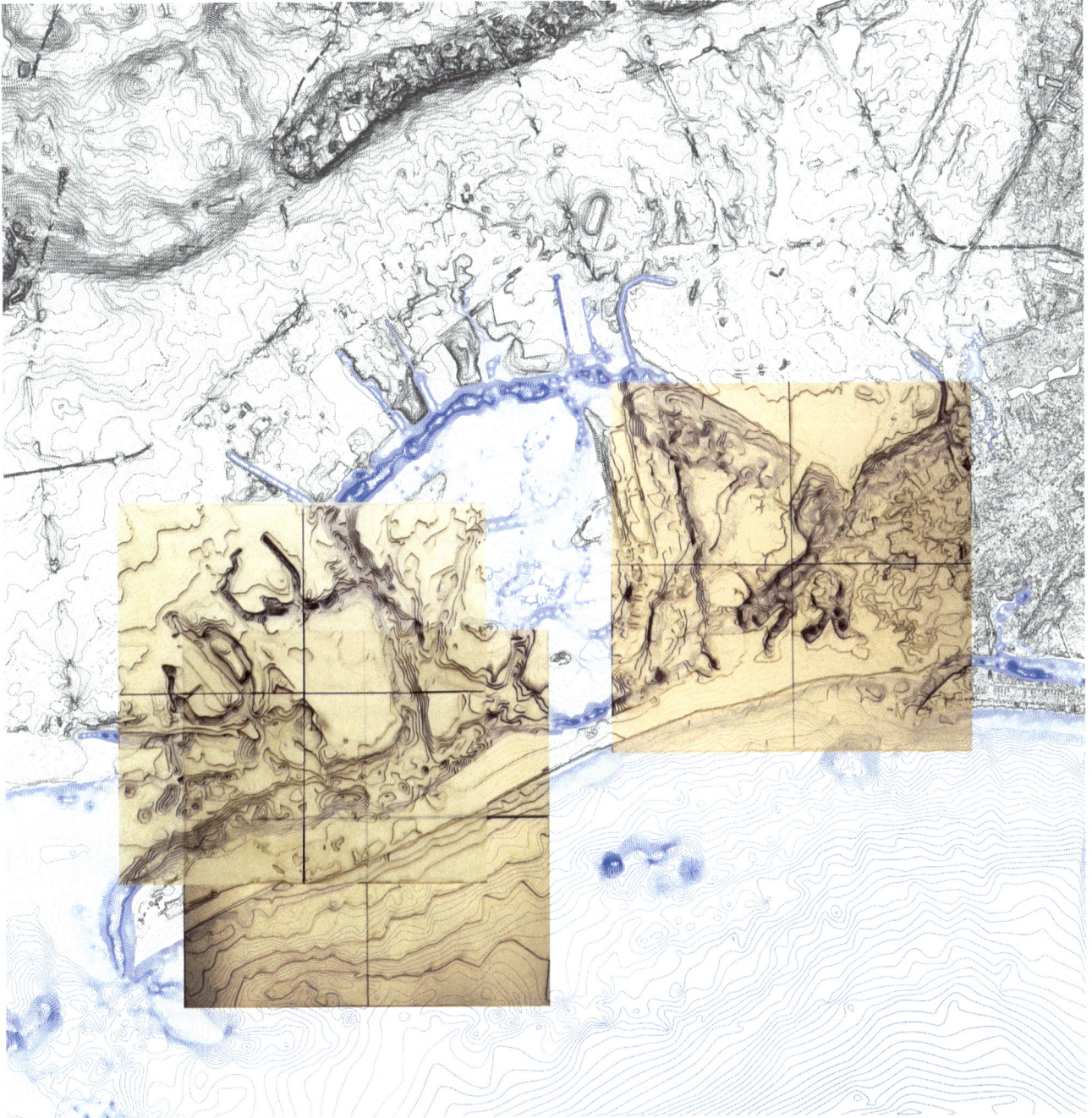

Topographic contours generated from the merged topobathy DEM are used to produce laser-cut topographic contour molds for casting

# TIMELINE OF HYDRAULIC PHYSICAL MODELS

| | SCALE VERTICAL / HORIZONTAL / EXAGGERATION | DIMENSIONS | TIME SCALE | PURPOSE |
|---|---|---|---|---|
| **MISSISSIPPI RIVER BASIN MODEL** USACE Waterways Experiment Station (WES) Study Area: 15,000 miles of the Mississippi River and its major tributaries, the Tennessee, Arkansas, and Missouri Rivers. The river basin model replicated 41 percent of the United States. | 1:100 / 1:2,000 / x20 | 200 acres total 20 acre fixed bed | 1 hour = 12 days | Test levee and flood control structures |
| **NEW YORK HARBOR MODEL** USACE Waterways Experiment Station (WES) Study Area: Upper and Lower New York Harbor, Jamaica Bay, and upstream along the Hudson River and East River. | 1:100 / 1:1,000 / x10 | .55 acres | 1 hour = 4 days | Fluid dynamics* |
| **SAN FRANCISCO BAY MODEL** USACE Waterways Experiment Station (WES) Study Area: Encompasses San Francisco Bay, San Pablo Bay, Suisun Bay, and the Sacramento-San Joaquin Delta, from Verona in the north to Vernalis to the south. Also includes the Pacific Ocean 17 miles beyond the Golden Gate Bridge. | 1:100 / 1:1,000 / x10 | 3 acres | 1 hour = 4 days | Fluid dynamics* |
| **CHESAPEAKE BAY MODEL** USACE Waterways Experiment Station (WES) Study Area: Entire Chesapeake Bay Area. 195 miles long, width ranges between four and 30 miles. | 1:100 / 1:1,000 / x10 | 8 acres | 1 hour = 4.2 days | Fluid dynamics* |
| **LOWER MISSISSIPPI RIVER MODEL I** Louisiana State University, Small Scale Physical Model (SSPM) Study Area: 84 miles of the Lower Mississippi River, from Myrtle Grove to the Gulf of Mexico (4,600 square miles). | 1:500 / 1:12,000 / x24 | .015 acres (20' x 20') | 1 hour = 730 days | Test sediment diversion |
| **LOWER MISSISSIPPI RIVER MODEL II** Louisiana State University, Expanded Small Scale Physical Model (ESSPM) Study Area: Currently under construction, this model encompasses the Lower Mississippi River region from Donaldsonville to the Gulf of Mexico, including New Orleans and Biloxi, Mississippi (14,000 square miles). | 1:400 / 1:6,000 / x12 | .25 acres (120' x 100') | 1 hour = 365 days | Test sediment diversion |

*Fluid Dynamics encompasses tidal patterns, current movement, saltwater intrusion, sediment movement

| MODEL LOCATION | MATERIAL | TIME OPERATIONAL |
|---|---|---|
| Clinton, MS (abandoned) | 10'x10' cast concrete panels | 1949 - 1971 |
| Vicksburg, MS (destroyed) | Concrete | 1957 - 1965 |
| San Francisco, CA (currently used for educational purposes) | 286 concrete slabs | 1957 - 2000 |
| Baltimore, MD | Masonite casts with hand sculpted cement | 1978 - 1981 |
| Baton Rouge, LA | Hand-formed template | 2003 - 2012 |
| Baton Rouge, LA | CNC-milled foam | Spring 2015 |

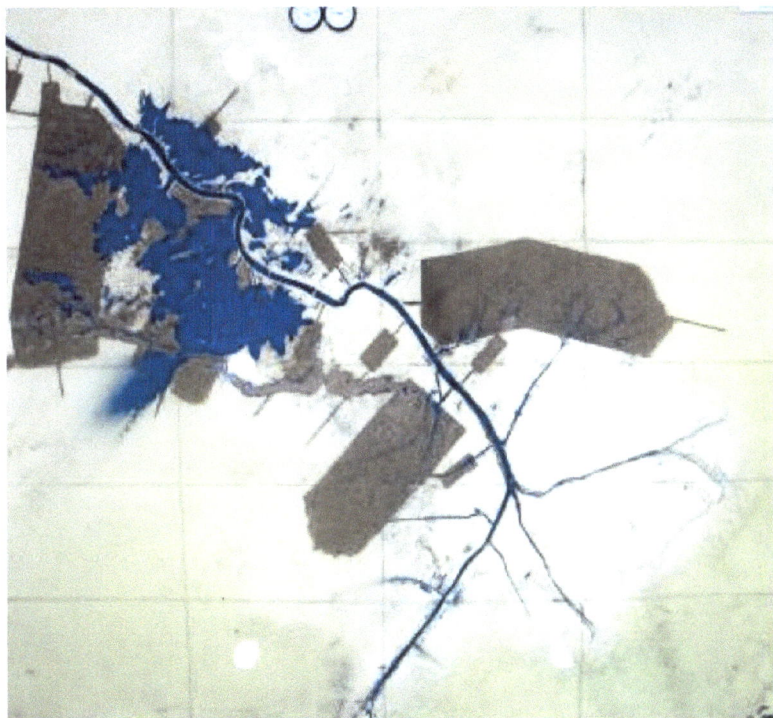

Lower Mississippi River Model I
photo: Clint Willson, Louisiana State University

MISSISSIPPI RIVER BASIN MODEL
WATERWAYS EXPERIMENT STATION, 1949-1971

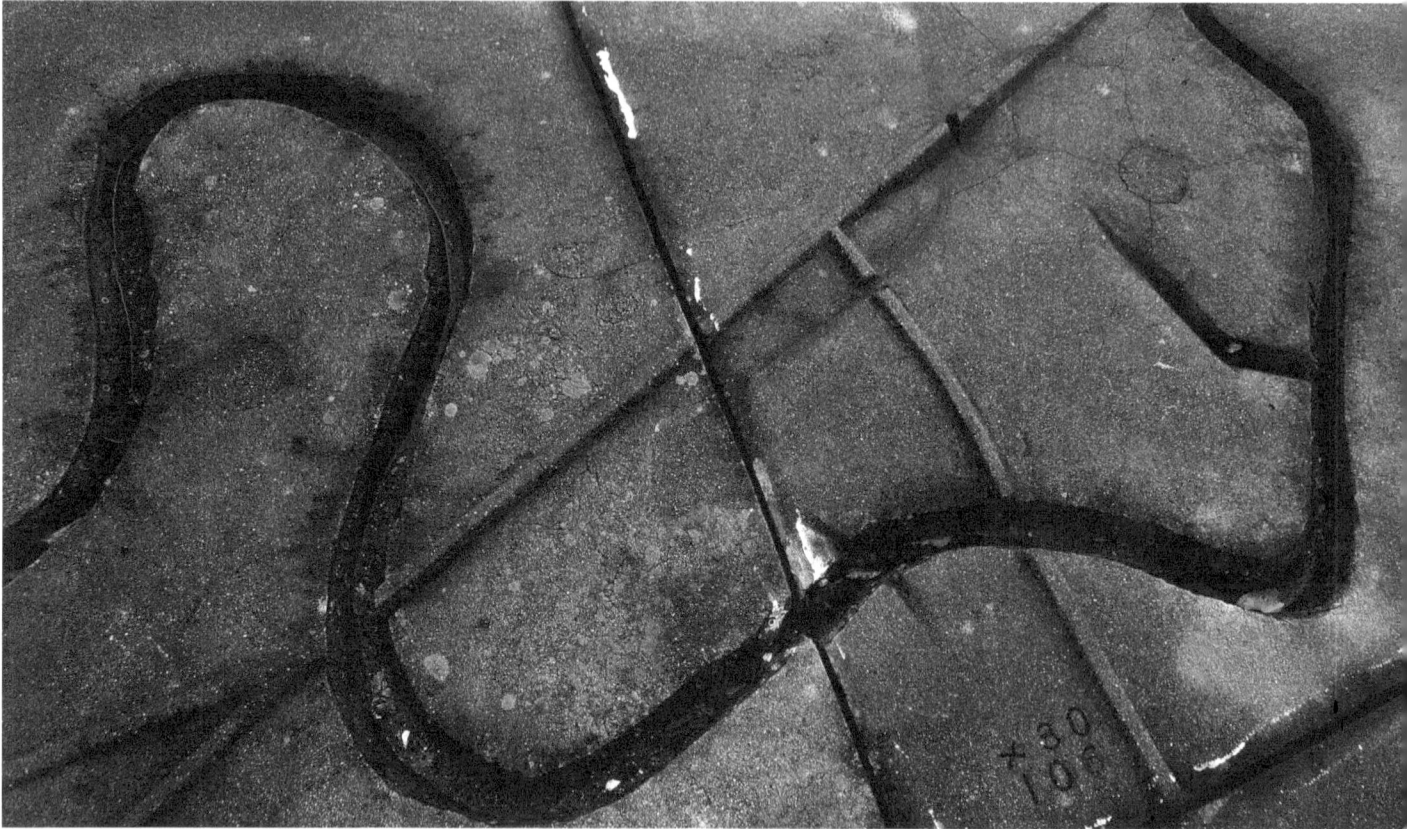

Mississippi River Basin Model (abandoned), detail
photo: Danae Alessi, 2014

Section of Mississippi River Basin Model (abandoned)
photo: Danae Alessi, 2014

## JAMAICA BAY WATERSHED MODEL

dimensions:      45" x 45"
scale:      1:36,000 (1" = 3,000') horizontal / 1:960 (1" = 80') vertical (exaggeration x37.5)
material:      1/16" chipboard
technique:      laser cut topographic contours (layered within watershed)

The Jamaica Bay watershed model extrudes the topography of the 80,000-acre land area that drains into Jamaica Bay, including much of Brooklyn and Queens as well as part of Nassau County, from the glacial terminal moraine to the Atlantic Ocean. The entire New York City region is represented, providing a scalar context to this vast area of influence.

Topographic relief model of Jamaica Bay watershed in context

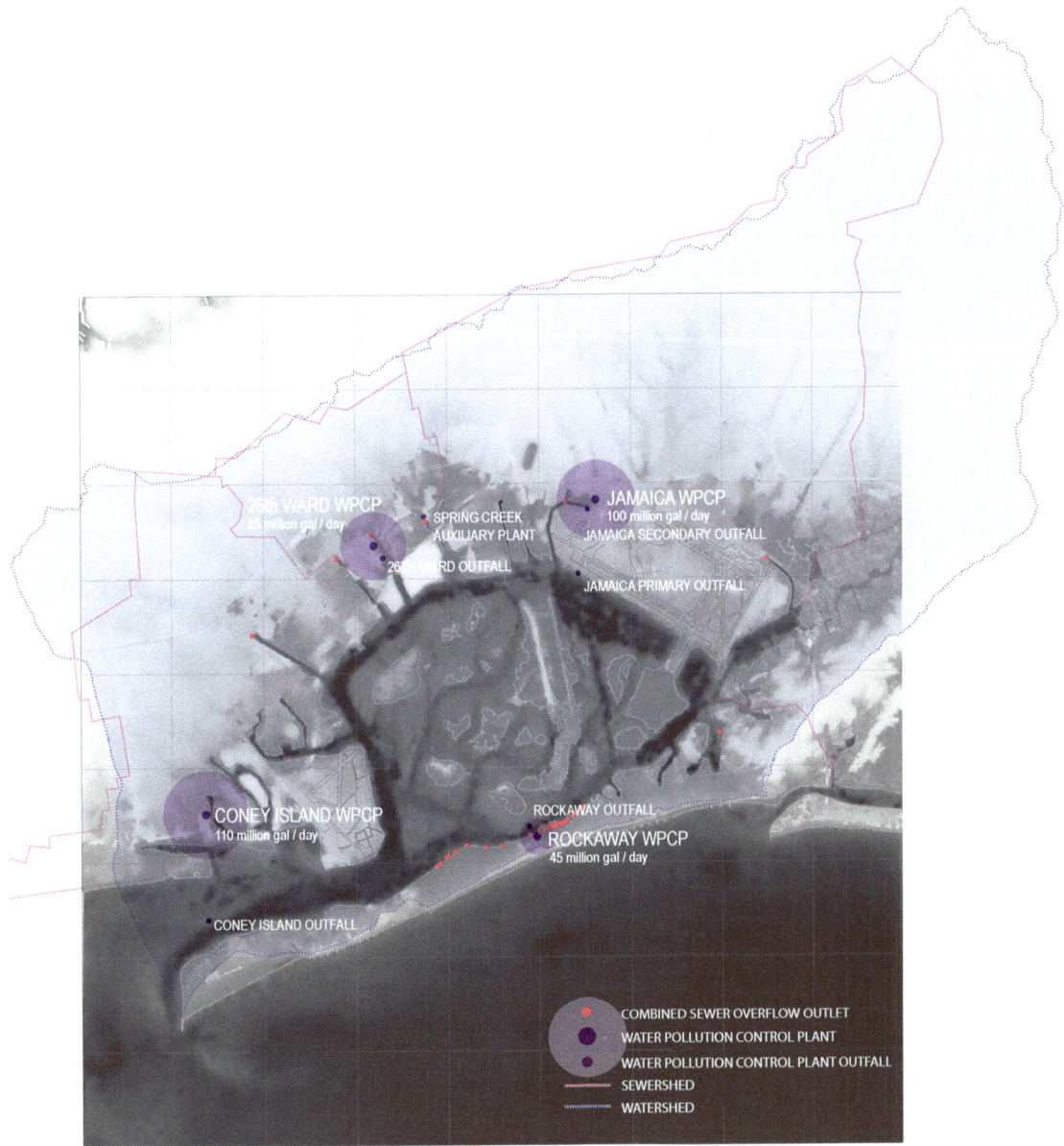

26th WARD WPCP
85 million gal / day

SPRING CREEK
AUXILIARY PLANT

26TH WARD OUTFALL

JAMAICA WPCP
100 million gal / day

JAMAICA SECONDARY OUTFALL

JAMAICA PRIMARY OUTFALL

CONEY ISLAND WPCP
110 million gal / day

ROCKAWAY OUTFALL

ROCKAWAY WPCP
45 million gal / day

CONEY ISLAND OUTFALL

COMBINED SEWER OVERFLOW OUTLET
WATER POLLUTION CONTROL PLANT
WATER POLLUTION CONTROL PLANT OUTFALL
SEWERSHED
WATERSHED

Jamaica Bay watershed and sewershed

## JAMAICA BAY TOPOBATHY MODEL

| | |
|---|---|
| dimensions: | 36" x 36" |
| scale: | 1:24,000 (1" = 2,000') horizontal / 1:600 (1" = 50') vertical (exaggeration x40) |
| material: | medium density fiberboard (3 ply, 1" thick) |
| technique: | computer numerical control (CNC) machine milled |

This continuous-surface full bay topobathy model is used to study the entire system of hydrologic flow and water movement in Jamaica Bay. Tidal cycles and surges are simulated to examine flow in and out of the Rockaway Inlet as well as overtopping of the Rockaway Peninsula. Injected dye studies are used to examine residence time, particularly near the deep borrow pits at Grassy Bay, Norton Basin, and Little Bay.

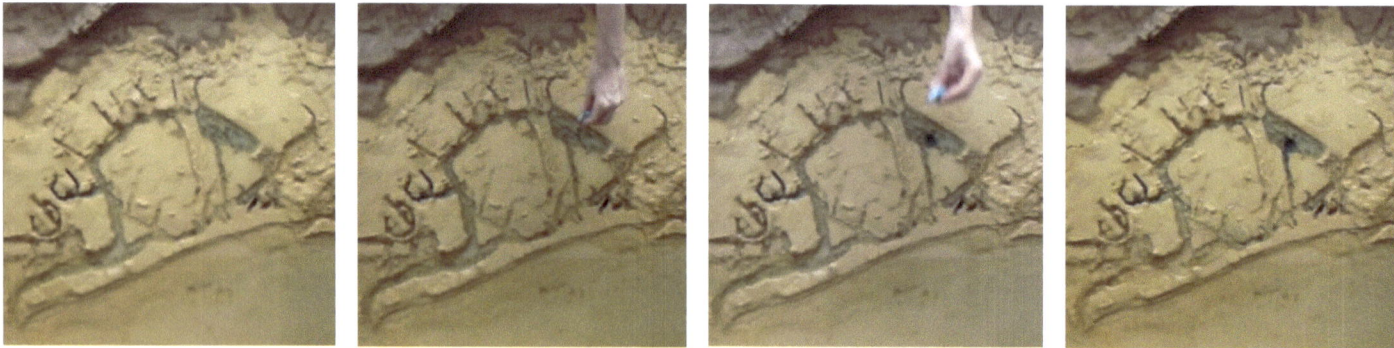

Topobathy Model residence time study, video stills

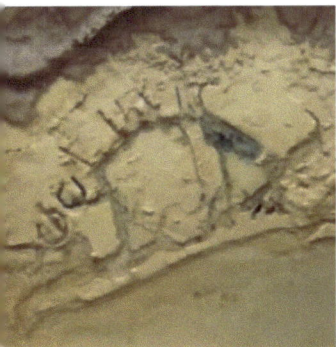

JAMAICA BAY TOPOBATHY MODEL

Mill Basin, Canarsie, and Howard Beach detail

Broad Channel and Marsh Islands detail

Floyd Bennett Field, Fort Tilden, and Jacob Riis Park detail

JFK Runway, JoCo Marsh, and Edgemere detail

# CAST SOAP STUDY MODELS
## CONSTRUCTION PROCESS

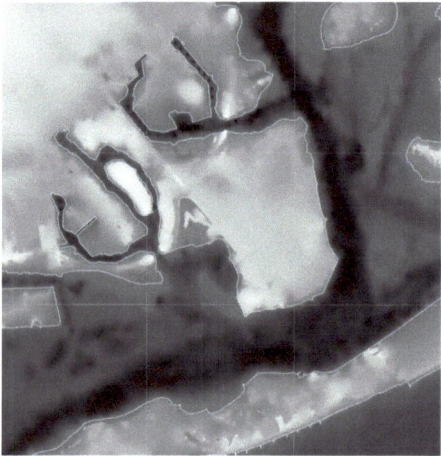

Digital Elevation Model (DEM)

Topographic contours

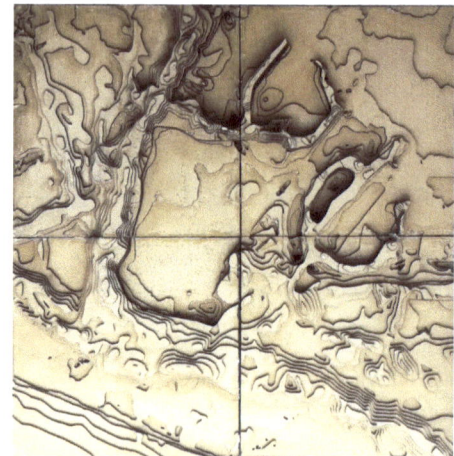

Inverse mold: laser-cut topographic contour model

Soap cast

Extracted soap cast

Water tank testing

## CAST SOAP STUDY MODELS
CONSTRUCTION PROCESS

Gluing and waxing mold in preparation for soap cast

Pouring melted glycerine soap into mold

Water tank setup with submersible pump

Extracting soap cast from mold quadrants

# FLOYD BENNETT MARSH INLET STUDY

| | |
|---|---|
| dimensions: | 24" x 24" |
| scale: | 1:12,000 (1" = 1,000') horizontal / 1:1,200 (1" = 100') vertical (exaggeration x10) |
| material: | 1/8" medium density fiberboard |
| technique: | soap cast from laser-cut topographic contour model |

Floyd Bennett Field was once a cluster of salt marsh islands including Barren Island, the site of several factories. It was filled to create Floyd Bennett Field and the extension of Flatbush Avenue. This hydraulic study examines the introduction of two inlets, one to the north and one to the south of the Belt Parkway interchange with Flatbush Avenue, to allow for the exchange of water and the development of salt marsh from Jamaica Bay's Mill Basin to Shell Bank Creek and Dead Horse Bay.

Topographic contours

Inverse mold: laser-cut topographic contour model

Soap cast

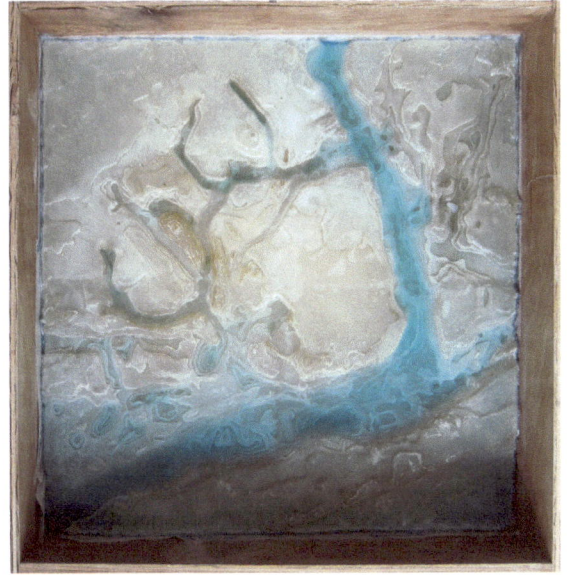

Water tank study

# FLOYD BENNETT MARSH INLET STUDY

Carving proposed inlet channels from soap cast

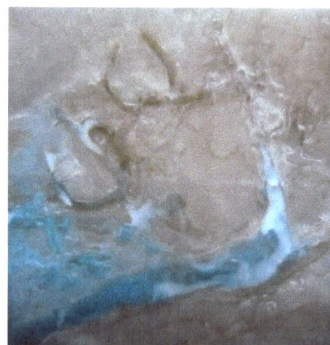

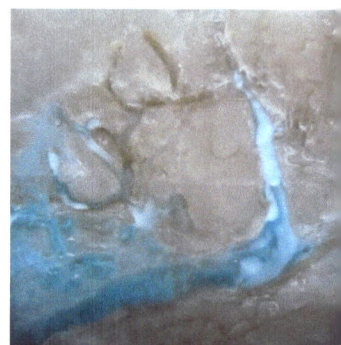

Floyd Bennett Marsh Inlet water tank study, video stills

Carved inlet channels through Floyd Bennett Field

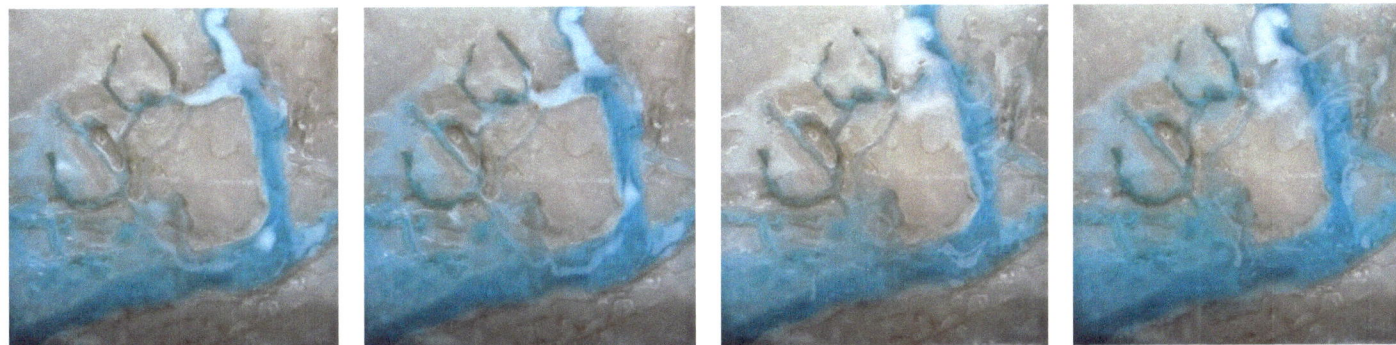

## JACOB RIIS OVERWASH STUDY

| | |
|---|---|
| dimensions: | 24" x 24" |
| scale: | 1:12,000 (1" = 1,000') horizontal / 1:1,200 (1" = 100') vertical (exaggeration x10) |
| material: | 1/8" medium density fiberboard |
| technique: | soap cast from laser-cut topographic contour model |

Jacob Riis Park, developed by NYC Parks Commissioner Robert Moses in 1932, includes a public beach, bathhouse, and enormous parking lot now managed by the National Park Service's Gateway National Recreation Area. This study examines the possibility of a designed overwash plain delimited by low earthen berms, allowing for the exchange of water between the ocean and the bay during extreme high tides and storm events. This exchange would enhance the delivery of sediment to Jamaica Bay, nourishing the salt marsh islands.

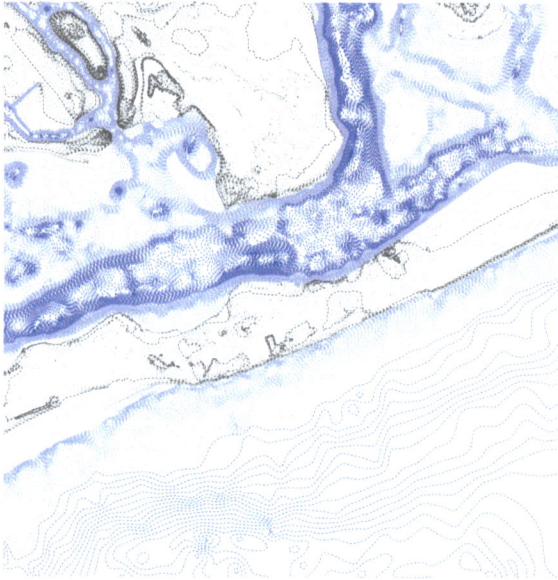

Topographic contours

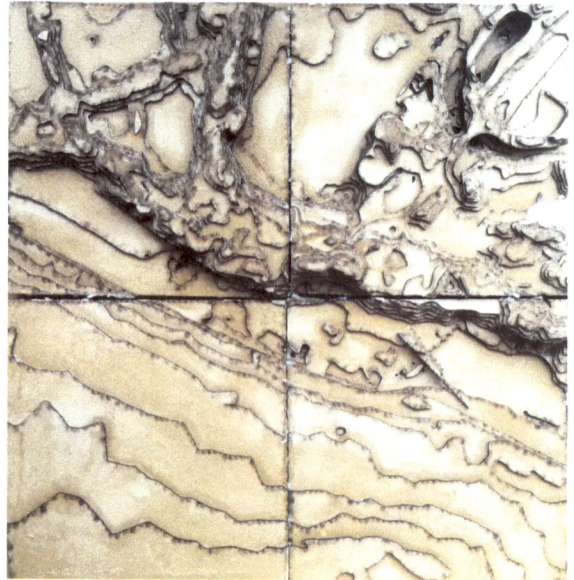

Inverse mold: laser-cut topographic contour model

Soap cast

Water tank study

# JACOB RIIS OVERWASH STUDY

Water tank study, Jacob Riis Overwash soap cast model

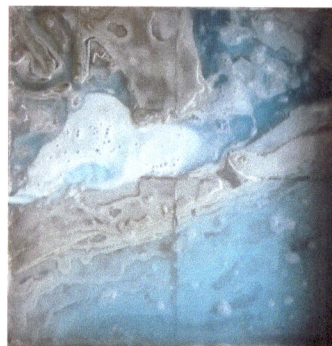

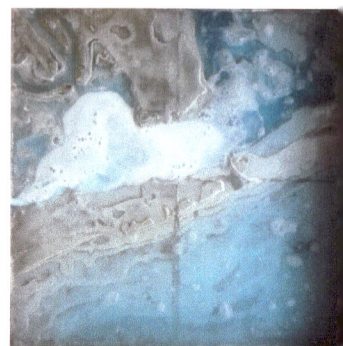

Jacob Riis Overwash water tank study, video stills

Jacob Riis Overwash Plain carved through Rockaway
Peninsula at Jacob Riis parking lot

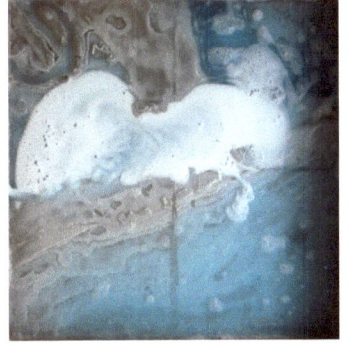

## EDGEMERE / JFK RUNWAY FLUSHING TUNNEL STUDY

| | |
|---|---|
| dimensions: | 24" x 24" |
| scale: | 1:12,000 (1" = 1,000') horizontal / 1:1,200 (1" = 100') vertical (exaggeration x10) |
| material: | 1/8" medium density fiberboard |
| technique: | soap cast from laser-cut topographic contour model |

The eastern end of the Rockaway Peninsula, including the communities of Edgemere and Far Rockaway, and the eastern reaches of Jamaica Bay, including Grassy Bay and Head of Bay, are often overlooked, but these are both socially and environmentally challenged areas. This study examines the possibility of transforming hydrology and improving water exchange from the bay to the ocean through the use of below-grade mechanized flushing tunnels.

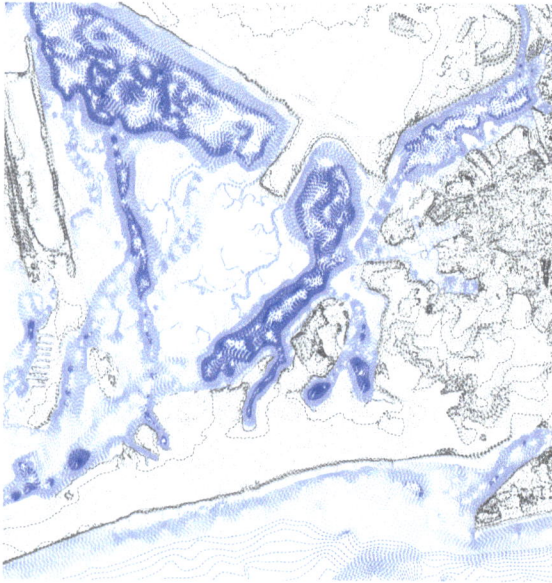

Topographic contours

Inverse mold: laser-cut topographic contour model

Soap cast

Water tank study

# EDGEMERE FLUSHING TUNNEL STUDY

Sommerville Basin, Little Bay, and Norton Basin behind Edgemere

Carving proposed below-grade flushing tunnels from soap cast at Edgemere

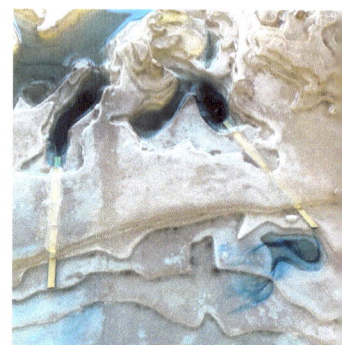

Edgemere Flushing Tunnel water tank study, video stills

Buried below-grade flushing tunnels

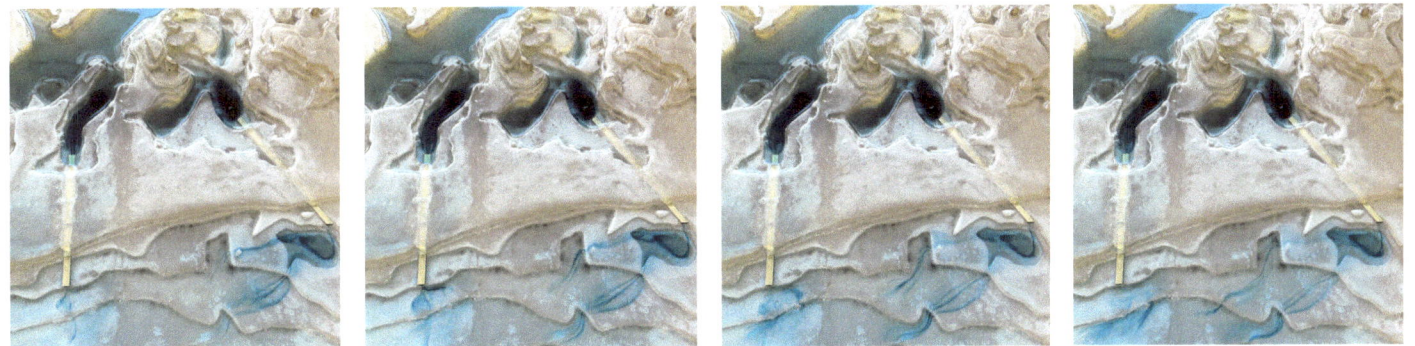

# JFK RUNWAY FLUSHING TUNNEL STUDY

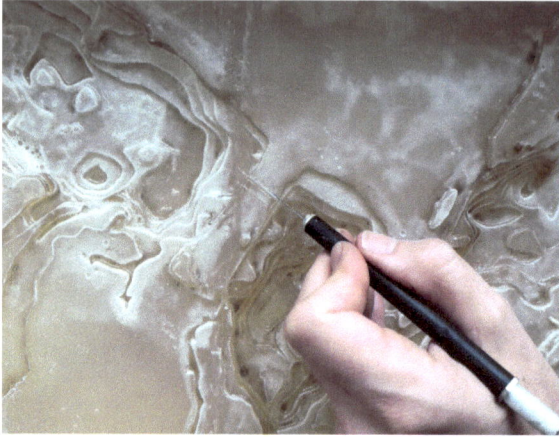

Carving proposed below-grade flushing tunnels
from soap cast at JFK Runway

Proposed below-grade flushing tunnels

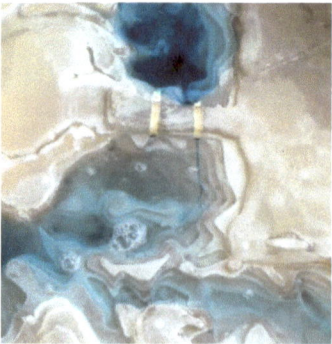

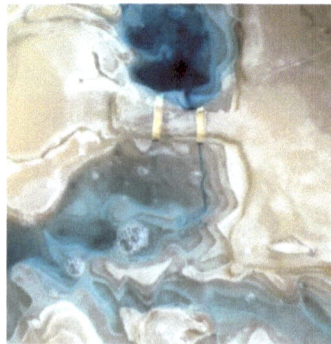

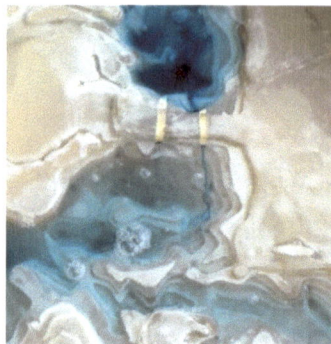

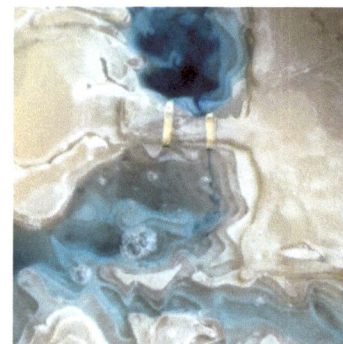

JFK Runway Flushing Tunnel water tank study, video stills

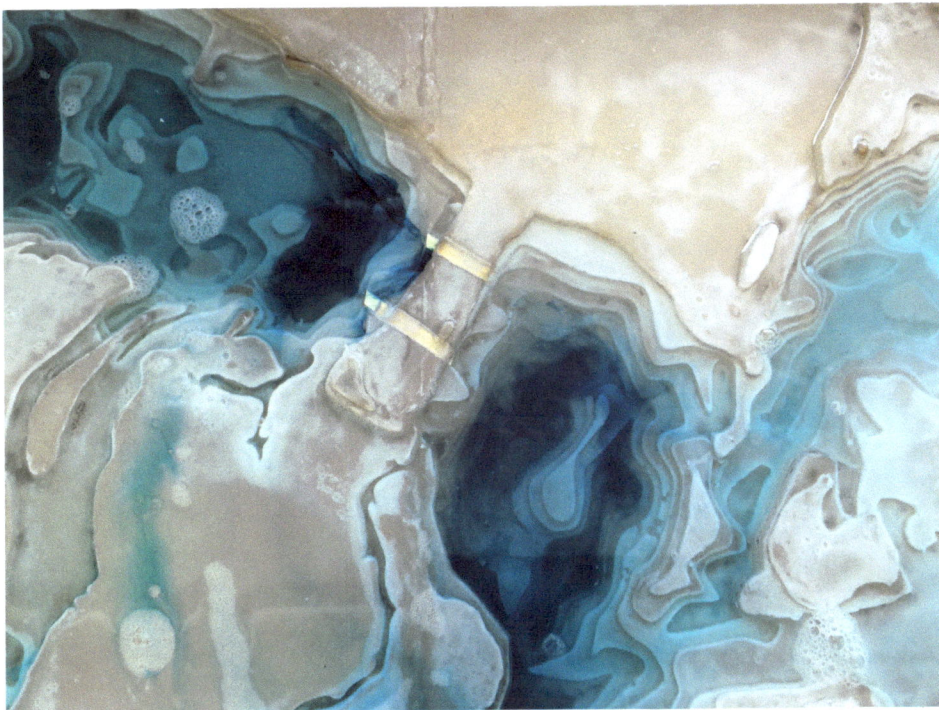

Dye flow test through flushing tunnels

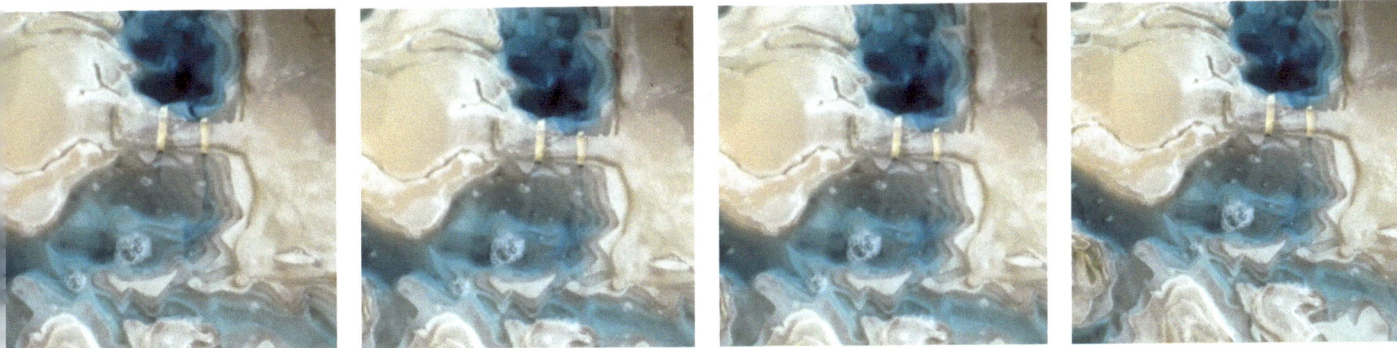

www.ingramcontent.com/pod-product-compliance
Lightning Source LLC
Chambersburg PA
CBHW060819270326

41930CB00002B/87